Time Management

Discover Powerful Strategies to Increase Productivity, Master Your Habits, Amplify Focus, Beat Procrastination, and Eliminate Laziness for Achieving Your Goals!

Steve Martin

Copyright © 2022 by Steve Martin - All rights reserved.

No portion of this book may be reproduced in any form without written permission from the publisher or author, except as permitted by U.S. copyright law.

Contents

Quote	V
Image	VI
Introduction	VII
1. Time Management: What Does It Mean?	1
2. Managing Time and Goals	7
Goals: Their Importance and How To Set Them	
Priorities: Define and Organize Them	
A Schedule: Create and Implement It	
3. Stop Procrastinating by Concentrating	20
Procrastination: Why It Happens	
What Are You Avoiding?	
Learn Why Concentration Is Important	
4. Free Goodwill	29

5. The Influence of Your Smartphone　32

    How to Stop Wasting Time on Smartphones?

    How Can You Use Your Smartphone to Help You with Time Management?

6. Effective Time Management Principles, Techniques, and Tips　40

    The Pareto Principle

    The Pomodoro Technique

    Time Management and Productivity

    Learn How to Delegate

    Effective Time Management Tips

Final Words　54

Image　57

References　58

"Don't be fooled by the calendar. There are only as many days in the year as you make use of. One man gets only a week's value out of a year while another man gets a full year's value out of a week."

- Charles Richards

Introduction

I was never one of those people that stressed over time but the need to increase the level of effectiveness in my career and personal life made me start paying attention to it. One day, I decided to improve my career level and prove to my boss that I am worthy of promotion. As you already presume, I requested far more projects than I usually take on monthly.

But as they say, before you eat the elephant make sure you know what parts you want to eat. I did not pay attention to the projects, or to be more specific, their requirements, importance, or duration. I just took them on and promised my boss that I will figure everything out at the end of the month. Guess what? I did not deliver a single project and I obviously only informed my team about it at the last minute. That caused additional stress not only to me but to them and to my management as well. And all this happened because I failed to manage my time well.

You see, time waits for no one—that is the hard truth. It is the only resource that people can't buy, borrow, or barter. Time also does not follow one of the main tenets of the law of supply and demand, namely, the idea that when the demand goes up to a high level, the supply will increase to meet it. Humans may use different amounts of time to accomplish tasks, results, and goals but everyone is given the same amount of time each day—24 hours or 86,400 seconds.

Over time, the behaviors that I exhibited, and that you probably have at times as well, are sure to cause resentment. This can result in repeated conflicts in the workplace, and at home. After all, poor time management causes stress. Stress affects our health and emotions and results in low mood and lack of motivation that additionally prevent managing time successfully. I tried to complete my projects at the last minute because I did not effectively manage my time. I sat and relaxed in front of the television without doing work, I was constantly scrolling through social media, and I waited until the end of the month to finish the projects I took on voluntarily. I sacrificed the quality of my work, I missed my deadlines, I caused stress, and I impacted others negatively.

Of course, I did not get a promotion. What I did get, however, was awareness. Awareness of a problem that I had subconsciously—my inability to manage time. I never paid attention to something that could make my future better. I realized that time is one of the top reasons for success or failure in my life. Investing bigger amounts of time into a goal, objective, need, or even weakness can tip the balance of success in my favor.

After learning how to manage time, I started achieving my goals way faster than before. I started with fixing the damage I had done in my workplace and I finally got the long-awaited promotion. I started being effective, I did not multitask anymore, and I focused on one activity at a time for a specified duration. I did more in less time by prioritizing essential tasks that require immediate action and by creating a proper schedule.

I wrote this book because I had walked in your shoes for quite a while and I know the pain that you are experiencing at the moment. How are you going to solve your problem with time management? You should do it the same way I did.

I am going to show you exactly how to manage your time. In this book, I will first explain time, its management, and its importance. Then, I will show you the negative side of procrastinating, of using a smartphone improperly, and how to get over them with the help of concentration and motivation. Finally, I will introduce you to some of the most important time management principles and techniques, like the Pareto and the Pomodoro principles, and I will end this book with some everyday tips.

I want you to know that I am going to walk you through, step-by-step, until you learn how to manage time. You see, this is not just theory; it consists of real techniques, tools, and strategies that I have personally used, coached, taught, and researched. They help you with your discipline, goals, values, habits, management styles, and persuasion. I've seen them bring forth a bounty of results in my life as well as in the lives of countless others.

As stated above, for a long amount of time, I was in your shoes. I had no idea about the importance of time management and the benefits that can result from it. I was stuck and I was not able to go forward in either my professional or my private life. I was suffering and I knew that I had to make a change. I am grateful for that change and I am proud of myself because I have been applying my time management skills for over 15 years now. They work and they deliver results.

Are you ready to learn about time management and the skills required for successfully implementing it into your life? If your answer is yes, keep reading.

Chapter 1

Time Management: What Does It Mean?

THE 84,400 SECONDS PER day we get may seem a lot but they go fast. Regardless of how quickly time seems to fly by for you, even the most skilled time manager's hours, minutes, and seconds tick by at the same rate. How do you perceive time? Do most of the things that you do daily feel mechanical and not personally gratifying?

People constantly look at other people and realize that quite a few of them get a lot more done than they do. That is not happening because they have more time but because of their time management skills. Without a doubt, managing your time will positively affect your goals and, in the end, your success.

Time is the substance of our lives. We don't create time in our lives but instead "create our lives in time." But people too often feel that, in their personal and professional lives, time is running them. They feel they only have time for one life—personal or professional—but not both. The difference in giving your time more meaning or making it more productive is not found in trying to speed up or slow down your days. It is what you choose to do within the time frames that constrain you that makes the difference (Cross, 1980).

Answer this for me—are you taking advantage of the time that is available to you? Some people seem to have been born with a natural understanding of time management. Fortunately for the rest of us, it's a skill that can be learned and developed.

"Time management" can be defined as the process of oganizing and planning how to split your time between activities. If you become good at time management, you will become able to work smarter, not harder. Learning these skills will make you able to work smarter and not harder and you will do a lot more things than before in less time. Yes, this will be the case even when your activities will be abundant and you'll experience pressure and short deadlines.

The people I mentioned above, the most skilled time managers, are able to manage their time extremely well. They use different time-management techniques that are included in this book because they improve a person's ability to function more effectively.

Let me put it like this. Senior executives and CEOs seem to possess unique time management and organization skills that enable them to dramatically increase their productivity. Indeed, people who are good at managing their time have strong skills in several key areas. They have a clear vision of their big-picture goals at work and in life —long-term, yearly, monthly, weekly, and daily goals. They are skillful at breaking these goals down into smaller units, and they know how to translate these small units into action-oriented to-do lists filled with tasks. Finally, they understand that achieving long- and medium-range goals means crossing off every task they can on their to-do list, every day.

Ultimately, how well you manage time boils down to your level of personal motivation. How willing are you to learn from the mistakes you've made about using time in the past? How willing are you to go after the things you know are important to do for the future? Most people know what needs to be done; they even know how to do it. They just don't have their priorities straight at the moment they make decisions about how to spend their time. Being more efficient in the present will help you achieve the future of your dreams. First, however, you need to motivate yourself to change some of your thinking and your habits (Cross, 1980).

To explain the previous sentence better I will include an example. I will dedicate this paragraph to the first real person included in this book, Benjamin Franklin.

Benjamin Franklin was a successful author, politician, scientist, philosopher, printer, inventor, activist, and diplomat. His accomplishments are astounding. He was a scientist known for his theories and discoveries and gained the recognition of fellow scientists and intellectuals. He was a political writer and activist and served as a diplomat during the American Revolutionary War. He was a newspaper editor and self-published author. Franklin started the first American library. His achievements go on and on. Benjamin Franklin is even credited for the statement, "Time is money." How did he find the time to do all this?

The good news is there is no more time! How can that be good news?

- In this respect, the playing field is level.
- Everyone gets the same twenty-four hours in a day.
- Your competition has no more hours in a day than you.
- The richest man cannot buy even one more minute of time in a day!
- You can only manage yourself and your own activities more effectively.

In a typical forty-hour workweek, it's estimated that the average person spends:

- 1.7 hours looking for things
- 1 hour rescheduling appointments and tasks
- 1.4 hours wasted because of rescheduled appointments and tasks
- 2.2 hours wasted because of lack of organization and priorities

This is a total of more than 6 hours wasted due to poor planning and a lack of organization. When people are asked why they are not organized, the number one reason given is:

"I don't have the time."

The fact is people choose to be disorganized. Most people could save this wasted time by spending just two hours a week organizing and planning. In just two hours of planning, you could free an additional three to four hours of prime time every week.

This book is about behavioral changes. Learning how to spend more time acting instead of reacting. The skills described herein will help you become better organized and manage time more effectively, which will increase your productivity if you adopt the behavioral changes outlined throughout this book.

Chapter 2

Managing Time and Goals

IN ONE SENSE, TIME management is about managing your goals. If you know what you want to achieve in the future, you can figure out how to use your time in order to get there.

These are the three elements of goal management:

- **Long-term goals**—These are the goals toward which you direct your efforts. Typically, long-term goals are completed in a year or more.

- **Objectives**—These are the steps needed to achieve a long-term goal. Objectives are typically completed in a month or more.

- **Tasks**—These are the series of daily and weekly actions required to meet your objectives.

To help you get the right things done—that is, get where you want to go at work and in life—it's important to line up your daily actions and your long-term goals. Thus, the first step is setting the right long-term goals and then making sure your objectives and daily actions support those goals.

Goals: Their Importance and How To Set Them

A goal is a purpose toward which you direct your endeavors. For example, your goal could be to increase your company's sales revenue by 15%. A soccer team's goal might be to win the yearly championship. A student's goal might be to earn an MBA degree.

There's an art to setting goals. The most effective goals are specific and measurable and should be motivating. If a goal is too vague—for example, the resolution to make your firm the "best company in the world"—you will not be able to monitor your progress toward that goal, or even know whether or not you have achieved it. Does being the "best company in the world" mean "greatest sales" or "a greater return on sales" than any other company? Does it mean that your employee retention rate is the highest of the firms in your field? If the goal you articulate can't be measured, take another stab at defining it (Eccles, Wigfield, 2002).

An effective goal is also ambitious but not impossible to achieve. For instance, a goal of earning an MBA within six months is not realistic; getting the degree within two or three years is reasonable, on the other hand. Assigning a reasonable amount of time for the completion of your goals is essential. Only if you've established a clear and realistic deadline will you be able to determine how to best accomplish a goal. How you define a long-term goal is, to some degree, up to you. Is it a goal you want to achieve in the long term or the short term?

Regardless of what that timeframe is, strong time managers break down their long-term goals into objectives. If your long-term goal is to finish a particularly complex project within a year, for example, your objectives will state what you need to do in the next month, the next three months, the next six months, and so on to meet your long-term goal.

To move toward achieving these objectives, effective time managers break these objectives down further into tasks—things that you need to do in the short term—within the week, the day, or the hour. This process of dividing a long-term goal into smaller segments is also known as chunking. Look at a goal as you would a big bar of chocolate. It's just not possible to stuff the whole thing in your mouth at once, even if that's your first impulse. So, you break it into pieces. First, you divide it into halves or quarters, and then you break it apart further into individual squares. Most people eat the chocolate bar a square at a time—and it doesn't take long for the whole bar to disappear (Eccles, Wigfield, 2002).

The most important thing to remember is not to obsess about your long-term goal, although you can think about it, discuss it as appropriate, and perhaps jot down notes to yourself about it on occasion. This will help you remember the direction in which you're headed as you focus on the chunks that you have determined will take you there. Keeping your ultimate goal at the back of your mind makes you understand the chunks you're doing at any moment and gives them more meaning than they might otherwise have.

Remain focused on implementation and action. Achieve your tasks and objectives, and you'll hit the big target right where and when you're supposed to. As long as your goal setting achieves the proper traction, you'll reach your destination, no matter how far down the road it is. When working toward your goals, remember the Eastern proverb that wisely state that "a journey of a thousand miles begins with a single step."

Dos and Don'ts

It's important to keep your energy and motivation high when you're trying to improve your time-management skills.

To avoid losing momentum, consider the following:

- Do write down your goals and post them in a visible spot where you'll see them regularly.

- Do remember what you ultimately hope to achieve. Keep your eye on the prize, so to speak.

- Don't forget why you're doing what you're doing.

- Do work with a teammate who will keep you honest about your progress and compliment you on your efforts.

- Do celebrate and reward yourself when you meet objectives and accomplish goals.

Priorities: Define and Organize Them

In our complex world, you can't wait until you have reached one long-term goal before moving on to the next. On any given day, you will be working on short-term tasks associated with multiple long-term goals and objectives. So how do you decide which to do first? You prioritize them.

But how do you decide which tasks take priority over others? Which tasks should be completed first, second, third, and so forth?

The first step is to have a clear understanding of what's involved in each task by asking the following questions—who, what, when, where, why, and how.

- **Who?** Who needs this to be done—your boss, a customer, a coworker, or a subordinate? Who will be performing the task? Who will benefit from this? Does the person asking you to do this task understand the demands it will make on your time and energy?

- **What?** What exactly are you required to do? Is it valuable to the big picture? Does the benefit of doing the job justify the investment of your time, energy, and resources?

- **When?** By what date do you need to complete your task? Do you have the time to accommodate this request? Former president Dwight D. Eisenhower explained that truly important things are rarely urgent and urgent things are rarely important. Unimportant things usually become urgent because of poor planning. Keep your priorities in mind as you take on new work.

• **Where?** Are there any geographic differences that will have an impact on the timelines of the task you've been assigned? Are there time-zone differences, for example, that will need to be taken in consideration? If you are working with someone in a different office, state, or country, do you need to consider the time it will take to send communications or documents back and forth between those two locations?

• **Why?** Why have you been asked to complete this task? Why is it necessary in the context of long-term goals? Understanding the big picture will help you stay focused and prioritize better.

• **How?** How should you complete the task? How will your completed task be measured or evaluated? The way that something needs to be done has a huge effect on time management decisions and on the quality and cost of the task.

Dos and Don'ts

If you are having trouble dealing with your workload in a reasonable amount of time, it might be time to consider these tips. Followed routinely, they will make a seemingly endless list of tasks more doable.

- Do ask yourself the basic questions outlined above.
- Do make lists and stick to them. According to experts, lists are one of the most effective time management tools.
- Do allow yourself more time than you think you need to perform the tasks you need to do. Don't let distraction sabotage your list of tasks.
- Don't forget to factor in time sinks like sending emails and returning phone calls.
- Don't fall into time traps like playing games on your phone or browsing online.

A Schedule: Create and Implement It

The second step? Creating and implementing a schedule. While some people are highly organized, many people are drawn into chaos by the demands of their work and of others. In fact, they are so habitually disorganized and stressed that they feel they cannot invest the time necessary to bring order to their lives, no matter what they do.

But organizing yourself and your time is not as difficult as it seems. This is done with the help of scheduling. Additionally, it will eliminate a great deal of stress. Scheduling involves creating systems that are consistent ways of doing things. Systems transform your daily, weekly, monthly, and yearly goals, objectives, and tasks into a coordinated whole (Cross, 1980).

For many working professionals, a day is an exercise in playing catch-up. You may be late for your ten o'clock meeting because you had to respond to an urgent email. The meeting itself runs too long. A crisis with a client interrupts lunch. Before you know it, three o'clock rolls around and you are just barely getting started with the tasks that need to get done that day. The secret to avoiding chaotic days such as this one is effective scheduling.

Not many of us know that there are many ways to look at time. Here is an exercise that will help you discover which time is more important to you.

Which of these are most important to you?

- Work time is time allotted to earning money.
- Self-time recharges your batteries and restores your physical, spiritual, and emotional well-being.

- Family time allows you to build and sustain relationships with the most important people in your life.

- Relationship time involves other people who matter to you—old and new friends, colleagues, schoolmates, and neighbors.

- Financial time goes to financial planning, investing, budgeting, dealing with bills and taxes, and so on.

- Community time is spent improving your community whether by volunteering at church or building a community garden.

- Education time is devoted to learning by taking classes, watching documentaries, reading, or studying online.

You might have other ways to look at time that are important to you, such as hobby time, exercise time, or travel time. Whatever they might be, understanding the different ways to look at time will help you manage it and balance your life more effectively.

Scheduling is all about being prepared. Most problems or crises you face on a daily basis are rarely that much of a surprise. You probably have encountered them before. That weekly ten o'clock meeting at work always runs late and that particular client always threatens to go to your competitor after receiving the first quotation for a project. Proper scheduling takes into account all your on-the-job knowledge and experience to prevent expected—and unexpected—problems from knocking you flat.

A good schedule is flexible enough to accommodate unforeseen developments and complications that can be anticipated. It should never push the agenda off track. A good scheduler always has a plan B. Creating a schedule that anticipates all possible SNAFUs is critical.

The first step to creating a sound schedule is assessing your to-do list. If you've ranked the items on your to-do list according to their importance, then you'll have a clear idea of what tasks absolutely need to get done on any given week. At the beginning of the week, take a look at your to-do list and estimate how long it will take you to complete each task. If you aren't good at figuring out how much time is needed to do various tasks, start keeping track of how long it takes you to complete each task, including any interruptions, and make a note to yourself for the future (Cross, 1980).

Once you've determined how long each task will take, plan the time when you will tackle them. Decide which day you will do item number one, number two, and so on, and plug the tasks into a daily planner or online calendar. Don't implement as many tasks as possible on the first day of the week. Instead, distribute the tasks evenly throughout the week, taking into consideration already scheduled meetings and deadlines for tasks.

Be sure to factor some extra time in the day to complete daily activities, such as responding to emails and returning phone calls.

Always allow more time to complete each task than you've estimated. If you think a project will take an hour, give yourself an hour and 15 minutes or even an hour and a half. Remember that it doesn't take a crisis to gobble up time unexpectedly. Activities you forget to include in your schedule will wipe out what you thought was extra time every day.

Dos and Don'ts

When you begin to make a detailed schedule, it is good to be aware of any pitfalls that may be lurking in the shadows. A good schedule is always prepared for and ready to accommodate surprises.

- Do be prepared for crises and unexpected events. Schedule time for them.
- Don't forget to be flexible.

- Don't neglect to have a plan B in case of unforeseen emergencies.

- Do assess your to-do list according to the importance of each task.

- Do become aware of how much time you need to complete certain tasks. This will help you better manage the time that you have.

- Don't try to get it all done in one day; instead, spread specific tasks over the course of a week.

- Do schedule time for thinking—a vital part of getting the work done.

Chapter 3

Stop Procrastinating by Concentrating

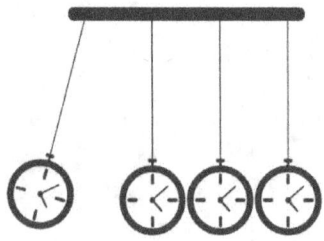

"PROCRASTINATION" IS DERIVED FROM the Latin verb procrastinare—to put off a task until tomorrow. But it's more than just voluntarily delaying. Procrastination is also derived from the ancient Greek word akrasia—doing something against our better judgment. It is a self-harming action towards the self.

If you're a procrastinator, then you've probably asked yourself at some point, "why do I procrastinate so much?" or "why do I keep procrastinating even though I know that it's bad for me?" These are important questions, since understanding why you procrastinate is crucial if you want to figure out how to stop doing it (Aquila, 1992).

Procrastination: Why It Happens

Although people talk about procrastination a lot, there can be considerable differences in what they mean by the term. Psychologists who study this topic make an important distinction: procrastination is a form of delay, but not every type of delay is procrastination. Before working on ways to reduce your procrastination, it's useful to understand this distinction and recognize times when you're delaying a task but not actually procrastinating (O'Donoghue, Rabin, 2001). For instance, you might need to delay some activities due to sudden changes in your situation or because you simply can't get everything done at the same time. So you might delay an activity to suit your schedule better. Although these instances involve putting off something, psychologists would not consider them procrastination.

Another particularly important distinction to make is between strategic delay and procrastination. The two are often confused. Strategic delay entails deliberately putting off a task as a way to generate time pressure as a source of motivation. Many people defend this strategy, saying it works for them, and some even claim it's the only way they can accomplish things. By putting pressure on themselves, they feel stimulated to work harder. However, it's a risky strategy because you might run out of time. It also consumes a lot of energy and can lead to a dip in which you feel exhausted after a deadline. What's more, there isn't much evidence to suggest it works by comparison to following a plan that is more balanced.

Procrastination is arguably even more irrational than strategic delay because the person will often be fully aware that delaying a task will have negative consequences, yet they still choose to delay. This is puzzling from a psychological perspective. For instance, even if someone has intended many times to finally file their taxes and they fully recognise it would be in their best interest to do so, they still don't do it. Instead, they start to watch their favorite TV series, perhaps thinking that they might feel more like it after one episode. But when the next episode is suggested, they start watching it. After that, they think to themselves, "It is really too late to start on the taxes now.

Tomorrow I will feel more like it." and then they go to bed. Procrastination describes this type of delay, where there is a striking gap or mismatch between your intention and the actual action you take and you feel incapable of overcoming it.

The psychological explanation for this common but irrational behavior is that, by avoiding the emotional discomfort of engaging in the behavior, procrastination provides temporary relief or an escape. The task might go undone, but at least the confrontation with the negative emotion is avoided (O'Donoghue, Rabin, 2001). Easier and more fun things encourage us to stay away, at least momentarily, from what needs to be done. This is the main problem: procrastination is avoidance behavior. It is the avoidance of something aversive by occupying your thoughts with something you would rather do that is available right now, not in the future. It can be seen as a conflict between what you want to do now versus what you should be doing for your future self. In short, it is a self-regulation problem.

Of course, at different times, some people might use both strategic delay and procrastination, depending on the particular activity. The key difference between them is the emotional connotations—that is, putting pressure on oneself purposefully versus irrational avoidance that runs counter to one's intentions (O'Donoghue, Rabin, 2001).

A common idea about procrastination is that it is triggered by fear of failure but we know that it is not just fear that leads to procrastination. Anything aversive can trigger it—boredom, resentment, difficulty, disgust, practically anything that is negative in your mind. Almost everyone has experienced needing to do something they would rather avoid.

What Are You Avoiding?

We are not always consciously aware of our emotions. You could use your journal to focus on when exactly you feel bad. Perhaps you'll see a pattern in the types of tasks and obligations that are likely to make you procrastinate. If you recognize a pattern, it might be possible to do something pragmatic about it. For example, it might be possible to delegate the obligation you inherited to someone else, organise activities differently, or have others step in to help you. Rather than avoiding it, perhaps you can find a practical solution to have the activity happen.

Once you get started, it can be helpful to manage your emotional discomfort by making the task more pleasurable, reminding yourself of its ultimate purpose and making it less arduous.

Learn Why Concentration Is Important

Concentration is the ability to direct one's attention at will. Concentration means control of attention. It is the ability to focus the mind on one subject, object, or thought and, at the same time, exclude from the mind every other unrelated thought, idea, feeling, or sensation. That last part is the tricky part for most of us (Howland, 2007). To concentrate is to exclude or not pay attention to every other unrelated thought, idea, feeling, or sensation. It refers to ignoring what is going on around us, the smartphone making the sound that indicates that we received a text or email, or the open tabs on our computer as we work.

Frequent distractions affect productivity. It takes longer to finish a task when you're not concentrating. You can't focus on listening. You don't comprehend things as well and end up misunderstanding, misinterpretating, and creating conflict. It affects memory. You forget things or can't recall information promptly, which affects your personal life and your professional image.

Factors that affect concentration in people include:

- Distraction
- Insufficient sleep
- Insufficient physical activity
- Bad eating habits
- Environment

All of these elements can affect your concentration. Happily, they are also all addressable.

If you frequently can't focus your thoughts and are experiencing ongoing concentration difficulties, this may indicate a cognitive, medical, psychological, lifestyle, or environmental cause. Depending on the cause, you may have to temporarily accept that your concentration is low and learn a few tricks to reduce its impact or accept the dips as they come.

First, you need to eliminate distractions. How do we focus better if we are always bombarded with information? Make a practice to block time in your schedule to do specific tasks or activities. During this time, request that you be left alone or go to a place where others are unlikely to disturb you, like a library, a coffee shop, or a private room.

Second, reduce multitasking because it is not beneficial at all. Attempting to perform multiple activities at the same time makes us feel productive. It's also a recipe for lower focus, poor concentration, and lower productivity. Lower productivity can lead to burnout. Examples of multitasking include listening to a podcast while responding to an email or talking to someone over the phone while writing a report. Such multitasking not only hampers your ability to focus but compromises your work quality.

Third, focus on the moment. It might feel counterintuitive when you feel unable to concentrate, but remember that you choose what you focus on. It's tough to concentrate when your mind is always in the past or worrying about the future. While it isn't easy, make an effort to let go of past events. Acknowledge their impact, what you felt, and what you learned from them, then let them go.

Last but not least, switch tasks. While we may want to concentrate on a particular task, sometimes we get stuck and our brain needs something fresh to focus on. Try switching to other tasks or something you love to do. Switching tasks can help you stay alert and productive for a longer period.

With strong concentration skills, you will start using every second of the day. I am ending this chapter with one simple exercise for concentration.

"Count the words in any one paragraph in a book or newspaper and then count them again to ascertain that you have counted them correctly. Practice this exercise every day for several times. When this becomes easy, try counting the words in two paragraphs, and later, count the words on a whole page. To enhance your focus and attention, count the words mentally, only with your eyes, without pointing your finger at them."

Chapter 4

Free Goodwill

PEOPLE WHO HELP OTHERS (with zero expectations) experience higher levels of fulfillment, live longer and make more money. I'd like to give you the opportunity to convey this value during your reading or listening experience. In order to do so, I have a simple question for you...

Would you help someone you have never met if it did not cost you money, but you did not get credit for it?

If so, I have a 'request' to make on behalf of someone you do not know. And probably never will. They are just like you, or like you were a few years ago: less experienced, full of desire to help the world, looking for information but unsure where to look....this is where you come in.

The only way for me to accomplish my mission of helping other people is, first, by reaching them. And indeed, most people judge a book by its cover (and reviews). If you have found this book valuable so far, would you please take a brief moment right now and leave an honest review of the book and its contents? It will not cost you a dollar and less than 60 seconds.

Your review will help....

....one more person to find a way to improve their life.
....one more individual supports his or her family.
....one more friend experiencing a change they would never have experienced otherwise.
....one more life change for the better.

To make that happen...all you have to do is....and this takes less than 60 seconds....leave a review.

P.S. - If you feel good about helping faceless people, you are my kind of person. I'm really excited to help you improve in the coming chapters (you'll love the tactics I am about to share).

P.P.S. - Life hack: if you introduce something valuable to someone, they associate that value with you. If you'd like goodwill directly from another person - send them this book.

Thank you from the bottom of my heart. And now back to our regular program.

- Your biggest fan, *Steve*.

Chapter 5

The Influence of Your Smartphone

TODAY, WHEN THE WORLD is globalized and fast-moving, it is impossible for humans to imagine their day-to-day activities without smartphones. They may be one of the most successful  inventions ever and have become a convenient means of communication. Today's smartphones are able to perform many other functions as well; they serve as music players, organizers, cameras, search engines, etc. Believe it or not, there are almost 6 billion cell phone users in the world (Kushlev, Leitao, 2020). I do not find anything strange here because people need phones in all spheres of their lives

—private and professional. However, if you ask me, smartphones are able to influence us negatively when it comes to time management. To be more specific, their excessive use is responsible for this issue.

There are certain harmful effects that are definitely caused by the overuse of smartphones. If you take a look at a few research articles, you learn that they may cause decreased attention, shortness of temper, sleep disorders, depression, headaches, and waste.

However, it is wrong to say that smartphones only harm us and waste our time. But I will focus on the negative side before I shift to the positive side of their use.

"Smartphones waste people's time." I do not have a problem with this sentence because this sentence is partly true. To explain it better, the times you check out your phone add up to an average of 90 minutes of phone time per day. In a year, that daily time adds up to 23 days and over your lifetime it becomes 3.9 years. Let's not forget that smartphones evolve all the time. They become more functional, and as expected, these numbers are going to become higher as time passes.

The question is: what are people doing on their smartphones during these 90 minutes, 23 days, and 3.9

years? Sadly, a lot of them are wasting their time. Do you wonder why? Well, the most used app category is social media, which makes up 14% of smartphone use time. TV, video apps, and telecom apps come in second at 9%. Communication apps come in third at 7%. Music, maps, and gaming apps come next. This means that for most people, smartphones turn into the ultimate time wasters (Kushlev, Leitao, 2020).

Smartphones' primary downside is their addictive nature (Kushlev, Leitao, 2020). A few years back, I became so addicted to texting that I decided to give it up—first for a short period of time and then forever. I decided to call people if I wanted to ask them something or to speak to them. I started to make plans to see them in real life without texting them. That is when I realized that nothing could replace face-to-face communication.

If you focus more on the topic, smartphones are addictive mostly because they are always within arm's reach. We should continue to enjoy our digital connection. However, our real lives are more important. Just like with anything else, too much of a good thing may not be a good thing after all.

Also, smartphones are likely to encourage mental laziness. Mental laziness is not a good trait when it comes to time management. Smartphones encourage mental laziness when, instead of doing math in your head or with pen and paper—say, when you're splitting a restaurant bill with friends—you may just use your phone's calculator instead.

How to Stop Wasting Time on Smartphones?

I am going to start this section with social media. As I told you before, social media applications on our phones are the most used of all apps and they are also the biggest time-waster when it comes to time. I am not going to lie to you, they are my favorite when it comes to keeping in touch with friends and family. I also use them to read blogs. But I was not like this. Before I realized the importance of time, I spent way too much time scrolling on Instagram and Facebook instead of working. Keep your social media applications out of sight so they are out of your mind. This is how I did it. I left my phone outside the room I was working in and I gave myself a few times each day to check my phone. I also tracked my time online. If you find yourself reaching for your phone every time it alerts you of a notification, change your notification settings. Restrict notifications while you are doing something important. Positive reinforcement is something that I have implemented on this journey as well. To be more specific, I set up a reward system—no social media applications until I do everything written on my to-do list for the day (Kushlev, Leitao, 2020).

Playing a few levels on a game that you have on your phone while waiting for something or while relaxing is not a waste of time. But, playing a game right after you use the phone to send an important message or an email is a waste of time. You are losing an hour or half an hour playing your game without realizing it. Trust me, I have been there and I know that you are doing the same thing right now. This is wrong and you should stop immediately if you want to manage your time well. The easiest solution is to delete the games that you have on your smartphone. But you won't learn about control in that way. Leave the games on your smartphone but do not play them while working or performing other important activities.

How Can You Use Your Smartphone to Help You with Time Management?

Now, let's talk about the positive use of smartphones. Smartphones can make people more productive and help them with time management. Remember that time management is not about getting a task done as fast as possible to the detriment of the quality of the work that you produce. It is about completing a task efficiently and effectively in accordance with the standards and objectives set for it (Kushlev, Leitao, 2020).

Your time can be easily managed with alarms and reminders. Alarms and reminders make everything easier because they remind people about important tasks. They also have the power to prevent people from thinking about other tasks because they force them to keep working on the current ones. Often, they serve as task-switching cues so that people can avoid the detrimental effects that multi-tasking will have on their management of time.

Schedules were mentioned in the chapters above, but I will dedicate a small paragraph about them here as well, simply because there are many applications available online that allow you to create daily schedules. It is actually quite simple. You need to open the calendar on your smartphone and implement tasks and appointments for each day. If you decide to do this, do not forget to schedule important breaks.

People can use their smartphones to create "to-do lists." They can also plan and write notes on the go. By creating an ongoing to-do list or a planning note on their smartphone, they have the ability to add to it whenever things pop into their heads.

Smartphones have the power to synchronize peoples' calendars, contacts, and to-do lists across numerous devices. For instance, people are going to be able to sync their smartphones with their iPads and home and work computers. This means that whatever people add to their smartphones will automatically appear on their other devices. Once you do this, you need to train yourself to implement every meeting, invitation, event, and deadline on your smartphone as soon as you are alerted to it.

Smartphones allow people to call other people all the time but this does not mean that you need to be permanently accessible. You should not answer your phone while working unless you're waiting for an important work call. Taking calls all the time is multitasking and it interrupts people. Additionally, it affects peoples' productivity. Turn your phone's sound off to ensure that you are not disturbed. This way, the caller is given the opportunity to leave a voicemail that you can deal with later. Alternatively, if you need to take some calls but not others, your smartphone can be programmed to ring if certain contacts are trying to call you but remain silent for all others.

It is important to mention that it would be foolhardy to expect to achieve smartphone use minimalism overnight. However, a combination of the above tips has helped me greatly and I am sure that it would do the same thing for you.

Chapter 6

Effective Time Management Principles, Techniques, and Tips

YOU CAN'T MAKE UP for lost time. You can only do better in the future. After all, you are here to improve your time management skills. Luckily for you, I know the best ways that could assist you. As I mentioned in the introduction, I know they are the real thing that could help you because I have practiced and implemented them myself.

Time management is not a talent that you are born with. Yes, you need an amazing set of DNA to do math like an expert or sing opera music, but with time management, you can work your way up to the highest level without having an "efficiency" gene. Successful time management is a matter of habit and it requires sacrifices and some specific principles, techniques, and tips. In this chapter, I present to you the best ones (Dunford, Tamang, 2014).

The Pareto Principle

The Pareto principle or the 80/20 principle tells us that in any population, some things are likely to be much more important than others. A good benchmark or hypothesis is that 80% of results or outputs flow from 20% of causes and sometimes from a much smaller proportion of powerful forces.

This principle should be used by everyone in their daily life. It should also be used by every organization and group. It can help individuals and groups achieve much more with much less effort. The 80/20 principle can raise personal effectiveness and happiness. It can increase the profitability of corporations and the effectiveness of organizations. It even holds the key to raising the quality and number of public services while cutting their cost. This book is written from a burning conviction, validated by personal and business experience, that this principle is one of the best ways of dealing with and transcending the pressures of modern life.

In 1906, Italian economist Vilfredo Pareto created a mathematical formula to describe the unequal distribution of wealth in his country (Dunford, Tamang, 2014). Pareto observed that 20% of the people owned 80% of the nation's wealth. He could not know it, but in time that rule would be found to apply with uncanny accuracy to many situations and be useful in many disciplines, including the study of business productivity.

In the late 1940s, Dr. Joseph M. Juran—a product quality guru of that era—attributed the 80/20 Rule to Pareto and called it the Pareto Principle or Pareto Law. The principle may not have become a household term, but the 80/20 rule is certainly cited to this day to describe economic inequity. It also is a useful tool to help you prioritize and manage your work and life (Dunford, Tamang, 2014).

How can you apply the Pareto principle to gain more time?

The Pareto principle, like the truth, can make you free. You can work less. At the same time, you can earn more and enjoy more free time. The only price is that you need to do some serious 80/20 thinking. This will yield a few key insights that, if you act on them, could change your life (Dunford, Tamang, 2014).

And this can happen without the baggage of religion, ideology, or any other externally imposed view. The beauty of 80/20 thinking is that it is pragmatic and internally generated. It is also centered on the individual.

There is a slight catch. You must do the thinking. You must "edition" and elaborate what is written here for your own purposes. But this shouldn't be too difficult.

The insights gained from 80/20 thinking are not many, but they are very powerful. Not all of them will apply to every reader, so if you find your experience different, skip to the next insight that does resonate with your own situation.

First, if you look closely at the items on your to-do list, chances are only a few are tied to important issues. While it may be satisfying to cross off a large number of the smaller issues, the 80/20 rule suggests that you focus on the more important items that will generate the most significant results. The list might not become much shorter but you will be practicing effective prioritization.

Next, in assessing risks for an upcoming project, you'll find that not every risk carries equal significance. Select the risks that pose the highest potential for damage and focus your monitoring and risk planning activities on them. Don't ignore the others, just distribute your efforts proportionately.

It is also important to note that the objective of 80/20 thinking is to generate actions that will make sharp improvements in your life and that of others. This type of action requires unusual insight. Insight requires reflection and introspection. Insight sometimes requires data gathering. Do this as it relates to your own life. Often, insight can be generated purely by reflection, without the explicit need for information. The brain has much more information than we imagine already.

The Pomodoro Technique

It may seem silly at first, but millions of people swear by the life-changing power of the Pomodoro technique. This may seem silly because pomodoro means tomato in Italian.

This popular time management method asks you to alternate pomodoros—focused work sessions—with frequent short breaks to promote sustained concentration and stave off mental fatigue (Cirillo, 2006).

The Pomodoro technique was developed in the late 1980s by then university student Francesco Cirillo (Cirillo, 2006). Cirillo was struggling to focus on his studies and complete assignments. Feeling overwhelmed, he asked himself to commit to just ten minutes of focused study time. Encouraged by the challenge, he found a tomato shaped kitchen timer, and the pomodoro technique was born.

Although Cirillo went on to write a 130-page book about the method, its biggest strength is its simplicity:

- Get a to-do list and a timer.
- Set your timer for 25 minutes and focus on a single task until the timer rings.
- When your session ends, mark off one pomodoro and record what you completed.
- Then enjoy a five-minute break.
- After four pomodoros, take a longer, more restorative 15-30-minute break.

The 25-minute work sprints are at the core of the method, but a pomodoro practice also includes three rules for getting the most out of each interval:

1. **Break down complex projects.** If a task requires more than four pomodoros, it needs to be divided into smaller, actionable steps. Sticking to this rule will help ensure you make clear progress on your projects.

2. **Small tasks go together.** Any tasks that will take less than one pomodoro should be combined with other simple tasks. For example, "write the rent check," "set vet appointment," and "read Pomodoro article" could go together in one session.

3. **Once a pomodoro is set, it must ring.** The pomodoro is an indivisible unit of time and cannot be broken, especially not to check incoming emails, team chats, or text messages. Any ideas, tasks, or requests that come up should be taken note of to come back to later. A digital task manager (there are tons of apps on the Google app store and the Apple store) would ease your job, but pen and paper work fine too.

In the event of an unavoidable disruption, take your five-minute break and start again. Cirillo recommends that you track interruptions (internal or external) as they occur and reflect on how to avoid them in your next session (Cirillo, 2006).

The rule applies even if you do finish your given task before the timer goes off. Use the rest of your time to learn or improve skills or the scope of your knowledge. For example, you could spend the extra time reading professional journals or researching networking opportunities.

The pomodoro technique can be a valuable weapon against the planning fallacy as well. When you start working in short, timed sessions, time is no longer an abstract concept but a concrete event. It becomes a pomodoro—a unit of both time and effort. Distinct from the idea of 25 minutes of general "work," the pomodoro is an event that measures focus on a single task (or several simple tasks).

The concept of time changes from a negative—something that has been lost—to a positive representation of events that were accomplished. I call it "inverting time" because it changes the perception of time from an abstract source of anxiety to an exact measure of productivity. This leads to much more realistic time estimates.

When you use the Pomodoro technique, you have a clear measurement of your finite time and your efforts, allowing you to reflect and plan your days more accurately and efficiently. With practice, you'll be able to accurately assess how many pomodoros a task will take and build more consistent time management habits.

Time Management and Productivity

With time management, every person in this world can increase their focus. As we all know, increased focus improves our productivity like nothing else. It also gives us a chance to capture bigger opportunities. Higher levels of productivity help you get more done in less time and significantly decrease the stress people feel when they have a lot to do.

When you manage your time, you can plan your day and increase your performance. Daily planning improves productivity as well. Planning your time is an important element of time management that increases productivity and effectiveness.

Learn How to Delegate

Track relay is one of my favorite sports to watch, especially during the Olympics. That is because the runners participating make blindly reaching for a baton at 20 mph while staying in their lanes look so easy. However, easy is not a word that describes the situation well. What they are doing is really difficult. The reason why I am impressed by this sport is quite easy to explain. These athletes know how to delegate effectively.

At first, delegating sounds easy, as we have already seen. When I first started organizing my time, I thought it was going to be a piece of cake. I was wrong. "Passing the baton" requires a lot of communication, coordination, and trust.

Delegation is important in time management because you should not do everything yourself. If you learn how to delegate, you will empower the people you work with or live with, you will build trust with them, and you will assist their development as well as yours. For example, if you know how to delegate at work you will do a task in a smaller amount of time. Also, you will divide your chores and you will lower the amount of time you spend on things like cleaning (Cross, 1980).

In order to delegate efficiently, you need to start with the right person for the job, task, or chore. For instance, you need to learn about every strength, weakness, and preference of the person you want to ask for help or assign to a task. Then, you have to explain to them why you want to have them take the task on. It really helps when you explain to people why you are giving them responsibilities. Last but not least, always say thank you. Regardless of whether the task is successful or not, show appreciation and make sure it is genuine and comes from the heart.

Effective Time Management Tips

The upcoming time management tips are crucial steps to stay on track. They are small investments that will pay out in the end and make you able to handle a full day of activities without losing productivity or a significant amount of time (Cross, 1980).

1) Take Care of Your Health and Decrease Stress

Taking care of yourself and your health will help your body rejuvenate, both mentally and physically. When their minds are healthy, people can achieve a lot. Practice managing your time according to your biological clock by scheduling priority tasks during the peak time of the day when your energy levels are at their best.

I suggest engaging in exercise. Do yoga, go jogging, or ride a bicycle. Every time you have done a workout, you will be feeling much healthier and full of new energy—ready to tackle all your tasks for the day.

2) Start Your Day Early

A lot of people are more productive in the morning. That is logical because, after sleep, people have more energy. They are more alert and ready to take on everything they have planned the day before. I do this all the time. For example, if I have one more project or one more task for the day than I normally do, I set my alarm clock a couple of hours earlier than I usually do. Mornings are way more productive for me than staying up late in the evenings. According to my experience so far, mornings can offer people a significant amount of extra time.

3) Always Plan

Every evening, take your smartphone or your notebook and start planning the next day. If this does not sound good for you or if it sounds exhausting, then try doing it every Sunday. Plan your days ahead, invest half an hour in this task and I guarantee you higher productivity and efficiency. While you plan, do not forget to:

- Review all of your commitments.
- Add every personal appointment.
- Add everything that you failed to do on the previous day.
- Identify your top priorities.

4) Never Forget About Your Personal Time Management System

Create or adopt a time management system that works for you. While crafting this time management system, make sure to take into consideration your priorities, tasks, personal meetings, work meetings, and goals. And most importantly, stick to it. Remember, if something does not work, remove it and add something else. This is another simple skill that will make you more efficient and bring a greater return in time.

5) Find a Quiet Place

Noise is not good for us. It distracts us and makes us unable to recharge and relax. When you want to concentrate, look for a quiet place or a quiet time of day. For example, I often go to the nearest park in the mornings to write. It helps me concentrate and accomplish quality work.

6) Say "NO"

Unless it is something really important to you, say "no" as much as you can. I started with saying "no" to tasks that made me feel highly pressured. I decided to save my energy and concentration for tasks that are important to me and I enjoy doing. You should do the same thing. Saying "yes" to a lot of additional tasks can make you feel overwhelmed and interfere with your time management system.

The above principles, techniques, and tips help you excel in meeting your goal and managing your time efficiently. They also improve the time management system process. In the end, remember one thing. Find the difference between interest and commitment. This way, you will become able to keep yourself healthy, stress-free, and organized (Cross, 1980).

Final Words

At the end of this journey, it is safe to say that time management is crucial to today's modern world. Without it, you will only function as a normal adult in a limited capacity. You will always be late with tasks and meetings, you won't be productive, and you will definitely experience chaos every day.

All that can be changed and this book aims to provide you with the help you need. At one point, we all get caught up in the moment and lose our ground, but once you have a plan to push you in the right direction, you will turn out allright.

The information that I included in this book, every principle, technique, and tip can change not only your view of time but also your bottom line and your life. Start every day with small steps. First, focus on what energizes you and makes you improve, even if the improvement is small. For some people, this will be the creation of a to-do list, while for others this will be using the Pareto principle. When you start with small steps, you will increase the chances of managing time effectively and you will feel in control. Of course, you will have more time for yourself and for those closest to you.

Furthermore, the strategy discussed in this book will help you stop procrastinating. However, do not over-schedule yourself. Adding tons of tasks to your day will lead to constant changes, delayed tasks, and feeling overwhelmed. As I mentioned before, take small steps when committing to time management.

Measure your success all the time and create a reward system. Learn from mistakes and do not repeat them. Adjust all the time according to your needs and your time management system's needs. Know your challenges and do everything in your power to prevent them.

This book is the first step towards change and a step closer to effective time management. Yes, changes sometimes can feel uncomfortable but we must focus on the bigger picture. Trust me, this step-by-step plan will help you become more energetic, profitable, confident, relaxed, and efficient. Do not forget to set an example for others. Tell other people about your plans and about your strategies. After all, every single person on this earth can benefit from this book by learning how to manage time.

If you enjoyed this book and the practical tactics I provided inside, your review is SUPER appreciated and will help me reach other readers just like you!

Remember, in a world where uncertainty reigns, contemplating the future with a time management system has a calming effect. Take advantage of that today and make your life easier.

Your Best Fan,
Steve

References

- Aquila, F. D. (1992). Is There Ever Enough Time?: Twelve Time-Management Tips for Teachers. The Clearing House, 65(4), 201-203.

- Cirillo, F. (2006). The pomodoro technique (the pomodoro). Agile Processes in Software Engineering and, 54(2), 35.

- Cross, R. (1980). How to Beat the Clock: Tips on Time Management. National Elementary Principal, 59(3), 27-30.

- Dunford, R., Su, Q., & Tamang, E. (2014). The pareto principle.

- Eccles, J. S., & Wigfield, A. (2002). Motivational beliefs, values, and goals. Annual review of psychology, 53(1), 109-132.

- Howland, J. M. (2007). Mental skills training for coaches to help athletes focus their attention, manage arousal, and improve performance in sport. Journal of Education, 187(1), 49-66.

- Klingsieck, K. B. (2013). Procrastination. European Psychologist.

- Kushlev, K., & Leitao, M. R. (2020). The effects of smartphones on well-being: Theoretical integration and research agenda. Current opinion in psychology, 36, 77-82.

- O'Donoghue, T., & Rabin, M. (2001). Choice and procrastination. The Quarterly Journal of Economics, 116(1), 121-160.

www.ingramcontent.com/pod-product-compliance
Lightning Source LLC
Chambersburg PA
CBHW071254070526
44583CB00017B/2460